If I Were God I'd Make Myself Clearer

Searching for clarity in a world full of claims

Also by John Dickson:

If I Were God I'd Make Myself Clearer

Searching for clarity in a world full of claims

John Dickson

matthiasmedia

SYDNEY · YOUNGSTOWN

Special thanks to:

Dominic for the view from the 'outside'
Cornay and Lorna for great suggestions
Harry for an eagle eye
Nicky for the welcome improvements
Richard for help with the finer
points of Islamic 'soteriology'
Rob and Kylie for the 'get-away' that got
the juices flowing.

For the Timmins family
in loving memory of Judy,
who came to enjoy clarity.

If I Were God, I'd Make Myself Clearer
Second edition
© John Dickson 2019

First edition 2002

Matthias Media
(St Matthias Press Ltd ACN 067 558 365)
Email: info@matthiasmedia.com.au
Internet: www.matthiasmedia.com.au
Please visit our website for current postal and telephone contact information.

Matthias Media (USA)
Email: sales@matthiasmedia.com
Internet: www.matthiasmedia.com
Please visit our website for current postal and telephone contact information.

Scripture quotations are from the Holy Bible, English Standard Version® (ESV®), copyright © 2001 by Crossway, a publishing ministry of Good News Publishers. Used by permission. All rights reserved.

ISBN 978 1 925424 50 8

Cover design by Judy Dao. Typesetting by Lankshear Design.

Contents

Introduction

I know of a teacher in an Australian private school who begins most mornings with 10 minutes of Transcendental Meditation, a few lines from the Koran and a rendition of The Lord's Prayer ('Our Father'). I suspect his motivation goes beyond that of religious insurance—covering all his bets, so to speak—but it is certainly an interesting approach to the variety of religions on offer.

By contrast, I've got a number of mates who do virtually nothing of a spiritual nature—no church, no prayers and, except for a few rugby matches back in 2001, no experiences of an ecstatic nature.

As strange as it sounds, though, both approaches are often just different responses to the one spiritual dilemma. When it comes to faith there appears to be no clarity, just a cacophony of competing claims.

The vast array of spiritual options leaves many of us bewildered, wondering which, if any, of these is rational, helpful or true. Some take the so-called 'pluralist' approach and accept all perspectives as valid. Others avoid religion altogether lest they be led up the proverbial garden path (others, I guess, avoid religion for fear that some of it might actually be true!).

This book tries to tackle the problem of clarity in a world of spiritual plurality. It is not intended to be a definitive answer—this issue is far more significant than a book of a hundred pages implies. Nor is it my aim to prove the 'truth' of a particular viewpoint, though I should acknowledge up-front that I myself accept the claims made by Christ.

My hopes are quite simple. It seems to me that most of us, whether 'religious' or not, have a hunch that there is more to life than meets the eye, as they say. And so I want to ask: what (if anything) has the Almighty done to match our hunches with something tangible? Because, to be honest, if I were God, I'd make myself clearer!

1

Incurably religious

A cultural eavesdrop

Late one evening recently I was enjoying the night sky out on the balcony when a fascinating conversation broke out among the guests of the dinner party next door—they too were out on their balcony.

The guests were your classic twenty-something Chardonnay-yuppies, and hardly what you would call 'religious types'. Nevertheless, at one point, the conversation turned decisively to religion. It started with one of the girls telling the others about a wedding she'd just been to for some 'happy-clappy-Christians', as she described them. A few lighthearted comments passed about the various Christians they'd come across, and then the conversation suddenly became 'deep'.

One by one each began to share his or her own insights into things spiritual. One bloke announced he preferred the New Age approach because it offered a spirituality that was meaningful but didn't make any of those onerous demands that Christianity apparently insists upon. The rest of them 'hmmned' in agreement. They really had my attention now.

The conversation floated from one aspect of

spirituality to another—the design of the universe, prayer, meditation, God, yoga, the church and so on. But there was one comment in particular that stood out for me as profound and quite self-revealing. One of the girls had made a sarcastic remark about 'organized' forms of worship—I think she was referring to the sort of thing I get up to most Sundays—and then one of her friends responded: "Yes, but there's *something* in it, don't you think? I like the idea of being grateful to Someone for the things in my life." It could have been my imagination, but the comment seemed to drop in on the dinner-party like a revelation: the response from the others was complete silence for at least two or three seconds which, at this dinner party, seemed like an eternity.

It was perhaps unethical of me to eavesdrop for as long as I did but I figured I could justify it as 'research'—something I may even be able to include in a future book. From the point of view of someone who writes and speaks on these issues, what struck me about this conversation was just how interesting and interested they all were in things spiritual. You could tell it was the first time they'd articulated their spiritual opinions to each other but it was equally apparent they'd all thought about the issues.

I came away reminded of something I've known for a long time but easily forget. No matter how educated, materialistic or secular our society becomes, questions of 'spirituality' just do not go away. We appear to be incurably inquisitive about realities deeper than our investments, our waistlines, our holidays, our retirement packages and so on. It is as if something in our world continues to seduce us with questions of faith—Why are we here? What happens at death? To Whom can I be grateful?—and a thousand other questions which have tantalized the human mind over the centuries.

This may sound like the wishful thinking of someone whose 'bread-and-butter' is the promotion of a particular brand of spirituality, but Australia's leading newspaper, the *Sydney Morning Herald*, ran a feature article with a similar observation. It was titled 'Highly Spirited' and it ran the teaser: "Despite its materialist veneer, religion is thriving in many different guises in Australia". The writer listed an array of spiritualities he believed to be alive and well in Australia. There were the obvious ones, Christianity, Islam, Buddhism, Hinduism and so on, but the informal expressions of religion were especially interesting: he pointed to the New Age movement, for example, and the modern fascination with Aboriginal spirituality.

But it is not just these obvious claims of faith that point to an interest in spirituality. I find it fascinating that some of the prominent atheists of our day have devoted much of their time and energy to spiritual questions. I would have thought that once you rejected the existence of God, and the spiritual realm generally, you would devote your attention to things material. This is apparently not the case. Philip Adams, for instance, the radio broadcaster and perhaps Australia's most vocal atheist, is constantly discussing religion—

usually with some scorn but frequently nonetheless. I once heard him debate a Christian leader on-air and his depth of knowledge about, and fascination with, things spiritual was intriguing. He confessed to having a particular curiosity with ancient Egyptian and pagan spirituality—not that he believed any of it, of course.

To offer another example, perhaps the 20th century's greatest atheist, the Englishman Bertrand Russell, was similarly 'plagued' by religious inclinations, even if in the end he was able to diffuse these with his rationalisations. In a biography written by his own daughter, Russell is described in strikingly spiritual terms:

> I believe myself that his whole life was a search for God, or, for those who prefer less personal terms, for absolute certainty. Indeed, he had first taken up philosophy in the hope of finding proof of the existence of God... Somewhere at the back of my father's mind, at the bottom of his heart, in the depths of his soul, there was an empty space that had once been filled by God, and he never found anything else to put in it. (Katherine Tait, *My Father Bertrand Russell*, Victor Gollancz, London, 1976, pp. 182-189)

Even late in life, after all his argumentation and vitriol against theism, Russell still confessed an unshakeable 'feeling' toward religion. After visiting an ancient Byzantine church in Greece, he wrote to his daughter:

I realized then that the Christian outlook had a firmer hold upon me than I had imagined… I realized with some astonishment that I myself am powerfully affected by this sense in my feelings though not in my beliefs.

Whether it's Chardonnay-pluralists like the guests next-door or hard-core atheists like Adams and Russell, men and women seem strangely drawn toward spiritual questions. It is as if we are incurably religious.

An ancient eavesdrop

Something similar to this was said almost two millennia ago in a famous speech by the Apostle Paul, the one-time-persecutor turned promoter of the Christian faith:

"Men of Athens, I perceive that in every way you are very religious. For as I passed along and observed the objects of your worship, I found also an altar with this inscription, 'To the unknown god.' What therefore you worship as unknown, this I proclaim to you. The God who made the world and everything in it… gives to all mankind life and breath and everything. And he made from one man every nation of mankind to live on all the face of the earth, having determined allotted periods and the boundaries of their dwelling place, that they should seek

God, in the hope that they might feel their way
toward him and find him."   (ACTS 17:22-27a)

This statement was made not in a church, or in a theological textbook with eager converts devouring every
word, but in one of the cultural and intellectual nerve-
centres of the ancient pagan world—the great city of
Athens. To be more precise, the statement was part of
a larger speech delivered (in A.D. 50) to the *Areopagus*,
an elite intellectual council of elder statesmen-and-
women which convened on Mars Hill overlooking the
old city. The purpose of this particular meeting of the
council was to assess the value, or otherwise, of the
bizarre recent news about a Jewish teacher in Palestine
who had reportedly been raised to life after Roman
execution and who, as a consequence, had sparked a
whole new religious movement. Paul was one of the
movement's chief spokespersons and so, in the interests
of tolerance, the Areopagus granted him the opportunity to explain the significance of this new teaching.
Paul relished the opportunity and in taking it up left us
with one of the ancient world's truly great speeches.

Throughout the book I will refer to this speech on a
number of occasions, giving us the opportunity to
eavesdrop on a debate which occurred millennia ago,
but which seems to me as relevant today in our
multicultural 21st-century context as it was back then in
the wonderful potpourri of cultures that made up first-
century Athens. If you're interested in reading the entire
speech in its setting it can be found on pages 77-79.

At this point, however, I am interested simply in Paul's cultural claim in the statement above. Not only were the Athenians 'very religious' but God has in fact arranged the times and places of human societies with the express intention that they should search for their Source of Life and perhaps "feel their way toward him and find him". The human family, in other words, is designed for connection with the divine.

Paul said this as someone who'd never travelled outside the Mediterranean basin. His personal experience of cultures was probably limited to Libyan, Egyptian, Palestinian, Turkish, Greek, Italian and, perhaps, Spanish societies. But all these years later, as we gaze down the immense corridor of centuries of historical research, Paul's words appear truer than ever before. Every single society about which anthropologists and historians know anything significant has made 'spirituality' a key component of their cultural life. Australian Aboriginals, New Zealand Maoris, native Americans, pre-Anglo Celts, marauding Goths, nomadic Mongols and modern Chardonnay-yuppies—every one of them has been, or is, conspicuously 'religious'.

It is worth reflecting on this for a moment. Talk of God is, in the truest meaning of the phrase, 'common sense.' Like the human fascination with art and music, or our desire for social organisation and personal intimacy, the question of God is one of the few universally shared premises of humanity throughout time. It is *common* sense. To ignore the question, then, or to relegate it to the level of the obscure, is to stand outside the mainstream of human thought.

Now whether this common hunch about things spiritual finds an answer in something concrete—such as an actual God, a real heaven and so on—is a separate issue. Paul obviously thought it did, and we will spend some time later in this book thinking about whether there is enough evidence really to support such a claim.

But for the moment, what is especially interesting to me is why we in the modern Western world talk about these things so rarely. Why is it that, despite the incurable religiosity of humanity, many of us talk about these questions only *very* occasionally, after a few Chardonnays, on balconies?

2

The attraction of distraction

Anything but the big things

At Christmas time, my wife (Buff) and I were invited to a rather posh party, sailing on a boat, enjoying beautiful food, wine and company, all while we watched the sun go down over the beautiful waters of Pittwater, in Sydney where I live. It was gorgeous. I met a friend of Buff's that night who in the course of conversation told me how well things were going for her. Her husband had just received a promotion so they were financially free, they'd recently settled in a nice home on the Northern Beaches of Sydney so life was secure, and the kids were all now at school so she could finally begin to enjoy more leisure time.

Then she paused and out of nowhere began pensively to say, "But you know, sometimes I really wonder if I'm meant to be experiencing more; you know, some sort of larger spiritual dimension to my life".

My eyes began to light up at the fascinating turn in conversation, and perhaps she noticed because as abruptly as she had begun she stopped. "Oh," she said, "but, of course, I don't want to talk about it; I'm really not *that* interested in it all!" And within in a matter of seconds we were back to talking about the wine and paté, and all the other wonderful distractions around us that night.

I had a couple of similar conversations that night. In fact, I have passing conversations like that at many of the parties I go to—and I almost never start them myself! For me, it's a classic insight into Western spirituality. You might call it a spirituality of *distraction*. It's not that we don't think about the 'great things', it's just that we find the distraction of the 'lesser things' easier to handle. Three out of four of us believe in the existence of God and the reality of the afterlife, according to the most recent research, but you'd never know it just listening to the conversations at work or in the pub, or to the public discourse in the media. We have this extraordinary ability to think big but live small.

In an interview with *Rolling Stone* magazine, the lead singer of U2, Bono, said he found exactly the same thing amongst his own peers in the rock 'n' roll industry:

> I don't know anyone who's not interested in the idea of religion, whether they're opposed to it or for it. Yet no one talks about. It's taboo. People will talk about penis rings easier at a dinner table these days than the idea of grace. (*Rolling Stone*, April 2001, p.58)

In slightly less colourful language, Richard Eckersley, one of Australia's leading social researchers, wrote a

Government report on trends in youth culture and described a similar avoidance of big issues and a corresponding obsession with small ones:

> When a society fails to imbue people's lives with a sense of worth and meaning, then they must attempt to find these qualities as individuals… Robbed of a broader meaning to our lives, we appear to have entered an era of mass obsession, usually with ourselves: our appearance, our health and fitness, our work, our sex lives, our children's development, our personal development. (*Apocalypse? No!*, Australia's Commission for the Future, p.14)

In other words, although we all suspect that life's meaning is found in more than a new wardrobe, a better car, a nice house, a fun holiday and a comfortable retirement package, we end up distracted by such things all the same. We are aware of a spiritual kingdom beyond the material one but we often settle for the material anyway.

In lieu of things spiritual

This devotion to things material instead of worshipping things spiritual is a very, very old habit. In fact, the Apostle Paul dared to broach a similar theme in his famous Athenian speech, calling into question a very popular custom of ancient Greece:

"Yet he [God] is actually not far from each one of us, for

'In him we live and move and have our being';

as even some of your own poets have said,

'For we are indeed his offspring'.
[*A quotation from a third-century B.C. Greek poet, Aratus.*]

Being then God's offspring, we ought not to think that the divine being is like gold or silver or stone, an image formed by the art and imagination of man."   (ACTS 17:27b-29)

Paul is speaking about idolatry, the ancient practice of paying homage to created objects in lieu of honouring the Creator himself. This may sound rather different from our modern passion for things material and, in a sense, it is. None of us is likely *literally* to bow down before our car, our wardrobe, our house or our investment portfolio.

Nevertheless, the similarities between ancient idolatry and the modern 'spirituality of distraction', are real enough. Both involve human devotion to created things rather than to the Creator himself. And, although our pursuit of the material is hardly a conscious act of 'worship' it is often a deliberate substitute for 'worship'. It's as if we hope that the accumulation of numerous smaller 'meanings' will make up for the lack of a grand meaning—as if the sum of the material parts will be greater than the spiritual whole.

It is a logic similar to this that led Paul on another occasion to make the same connection between the pursuit of material wealth and the Greek practice of worshipping idols. To a group of early believers in Western Turkey he once wrote:

> Put to death therefore what is earthly in you:
> immorality, impurity, passion, evil desire, and
> *covetousness, which is idolatry.*   (COLOSSIANS 3:5)

'Covetousness' (the pursuit of material things) and 'idolatry' (the reverencing of material things) are not so different after all, especially when they are a substitute for honouring the Creator of all things himself.

All of this makes me wonder how the Creator, assuming the Creator exists, feels about being replaced in the hearts of men and women by mere *created* things. We often think that what upsets God most are our individual vices—swearing, getting drunk, illicit sex and so on—but one of the grand themes of the Bible is that God is disturbed most by the way human beings suppress their hunches about his presence in favour of an approach to life that pretends he is not there after all: knowing we're mortal but living as though we're immortal; agreeing there's more to life than material possessions but settling for them all the same; admitting God's existence in the world but refusing his influence in our lives; having a sixth sense about God's kingdom but preferring the taste, touch, sight, sound and smell of our own private little king-doms. This, according to the tradition of which Paul was a part, is at the heart of what the Bible means by that unnerving theological term, 'sin'. Whether it's modern materialism or ancient idolatry, replacing *God* with *things* is highly irrational and, worse, culpable, which is probably why Paul brought his speech to a close with the words:

> "The times of ignorance God overlooked, but now he commands all people everywhere to repent, because he has fixed a day on which he will judge the world in righteousness."
>
> (ACTS 17:30-31a)

Living larger

Having said all this, the curious spiritual connection between materialism and idol worship, and the way these both serve as examples of what the Bible means by 'sin', are not really my concerns at this point. I am simply trying to underline something which is probably obvious to most readers: despite the sixth sense many of us have that there is probably a larger spiritual reality to be reckoned with, our society appears to prefer experiencing the smaller things of life with the other five senses.

Perhaps an analogy will help. Suppose I were an expert hypnotist and were able to convince you through hypnosis that the room you are presently in (if you're outside, please use your imagination) is the sum total of reality, that nothing exists outside the four walls. If you came to believe this suggestion, even for just a few minutes, instantly your life would shrink. Your hopes, dreams, concerns, troubles, desires would be limited to the items before you. Your social network would evaporate, your fashion sense would be reduced to what you are wearing right now and, assuming you're not in the kitchen, your culinary interests would disappear. Life, in other words, would become incredibly small.

Every now and then you might see a ray of sunlight through the window, or hear a voice, car or bird passing by. It might make you wonder for a moment whether the room is all there is after all, whether perhaps there is not a larger reality to enjoy. But, of course, if my powers of suggestion were strong enough, such hunches would be suppressed; you'd explain them away as wishful thinking.

I'm sure you can see where I'm going with the analogy. Think for a moment about how many times a day, through the media, the education system and our political discourse, we hear the message: "Life is about the job, the car, the house, the clothes, the investments, the retirement package, and so on." The repetition is hypnotic. Although few of us would actually believe such a message, hearing it so often encourages us to live as though it were true even when we suspect it is not. Any hunches we have that there is more to life than the material are set aside as wishful thinking or, worse, as weakness.

I suppose one of the purposes of this book is to draw attention to the sunlight and sounds coming from outside the room, so to speak, to invite us all to pursue the hunch and see where it leads. For it seems to me that it would be something of a tragedy if we were to confine ourselves to a small domain of life when there is so much more to enjoy.

But the problem of course is that there are so many different 'sounds' coming from outside, each with its own particular spin on what makes life truly spiritual. Sure, many of us have hunches about a reality outside the material one, but how on earth can one find clarity amid the noise of competing religious claims?

This is the question I want to confront in the rest of the book. It's not an easy one, and I don't intend to give a comprehensive or definitive answer. Fortunately, however, Paul's ancient speech to the Athenians offers some very relevant insights into this modern problem which has come to be called 'pluralism'.

3

An unknown God

God is what you make her

When in Nashville in the U.S. several years ago I had the misfortune of turning on the TV only to be greeted by the classic all-American tele-evangelist, the kind Steve Martin played in *Leap of Faith*—except this guy was for real, or would have us believe so anyway. "God is a God of prosperity," was his thundering message, "and he wants to bless every area of your life." He had a special offer the day I was watching. Viewers could write to him with their prayer requests—to which he would give his personal attention—and in return he would send them a 'prayer' cloth, a tea-towel size piece of cloth which he had 'blessed'. Placed in your car, the prayer-cloth would gain you the car of your dreams. Placed in the house, it would guarantee you the house of your dreams, and so on. Believe it or not, this prayer cloth was "Free of charge with every $1000 donation", because God was a "God of prosperity". The magic obviously worked because in the course of the program he showed us footage of his own home and cars!

Contrast this picture of God with that of Sonia, a young woman who had recently 'found religion' after hearing a message similar to that of the TV evangelist. People had told her that 'if only she believed' the Lord would fix her troubles which, in Sonia's case, were considerable. She did 'believe' (who wouldn't with a deal like that!) only to see her fiancé a few days later end his own life. For her, God was not a 'God of prosperity' but a cruel tyrant and a player of sick jokes.

The examples are extreme but they illustrate a significant problem of spirituality. God appears to be what you make him, or her. Those whose lives have been blessed with many fortunes will, if they think of God at all, imagine the divine being in friendly colours. Those who have not been so lucky may think of him in shades of black and grey. Some, like the woman I overheard on the balcony next door, will feel attracted to the notion of being thankful to an Almighty God. Others, like one of her friends that night, will baulk at the prospect of a personally involved being, preferring instead the 'Buddhist approach' (as he understood it) of a spirituality without demands. The options appear endless.

God in many guises

Some look at this array of spiritual viewpoints and dismiss them all, concluding that spirituality is merely a matter of style or preference, a projection of our imagination and not a fact of the real world.

Others—the great majority I suspect—adopt a more positive approach. Rather than rejecting all the options, they *affirm* them, suggesting that the spiritual traditions of the world in the end point to one unified reality: different paths up the same mountain. 'Pluralism' is the technical term for this point of view.

This was very much the cultural context of Paul's speech in ancient Athens. We often suppose that 'back in those days' the options were simple: society was mono-cultural and so decisions were black and white. But that couldn't be further from the truth. First-century Athens was a magnet for all kinds of religious claims from around the Roman empire and beyond. If you had a vision, an enlightenment or a dictation from a god, this was one town in which you could be guaranteed a hearing. The ancient narrator (Luke, of 'the Gospel of Luke' fame) who introduces Paul's speech states:

> Now all the Athenians and the foreigners who
> lived there would spend their time in nothing
> except telling or hearing something new.
>
> (ACTS 17:21)

The words are somewhat hyperbolic but the sentiment is nonetheless true. Athens was a city of great intellectual and spiritual open-mindedness. Paul himself, in the opening words of his address, acknowledges the same thing:

> "Men of Athens, I perceive that in every way
> you are very religious. For as I passed along
> and observed the objects of your worship,
> I found also an altar with this inscription,

'To the unknown god.' What therefore you worship as unknown, this I proclaim to you."

(ACTS 17:22b-23)

So keen were the Athenians to affirm all spiritual viewpoints they even erected an altar to 'an unknown god' (other ancient writers confirm that there were several such altars). Whether this was out of deference for gods whose names had been lost from the cultural memory, or a covering of Athens' 'spiritual bets'—just in case the known gods proved false or powerless—is difficult to tell. Whatever the reasons, altars dedicated to gods unknown is a clear indication of the pluralistic spirit which pervaded much of the ancient world and especially ancient Greece.

Living in Sydney, I was brought up in a similar spirit. I love the fact that I can walk down a main street in the city and, in the space of five minutes, pass people from a multitude of cultural and religious backgrounds. Some perhaps find this disturbing but I find it enriching, both culturally—my taste buds have never been happier—and spiritually—there's nothing like speaking with a Muslim or a Buddhist to help you see your own faith in a fresh light.

The great benefit of a 'pluralistic' way of looking at spirituality is that it promotes tolerance among peoples. If one person can believe in Allah and another in Krishna without coming to blows, that has to be a good thing. The bloody trail of religious history is enough to sour anyone's taste for monopolistic religious fervour.

Pluralism's fatal flaw

There is a real problem, though, with the pluralistic spirit of ancient Athens and modern Western societies. Sometimes, in seeking to affirm all religious perspectives, we actually honour none of them. For by insisting upon the ultimate unity of the faiths we often ignore and suppress what is distinctive about them and so end up sacrificing intellectual integrity upon the altar of cultural 'tolerance'. Let me explain.

For the most part, the religious traditions of the world make claims which are entirely at odds with each other. Superficially, the various faiths agree—most of them, for instance, say prayers—but at the more basic level they tend to refute each other.

Take the Eastern examples of Hinduism, Sikhism and Buddhism. Hinduism is premised on the existence of a vast array of gods (polytheism), each with its particular role to play and expectations of the faithful. Guru Nanak, however, a one-time devout Hindu and founder of the Sikh faith, came to reject this polytheism and insisted instead that there was just one deity who alone is worthy of worship. Siddhartha Gautama (the Buddha), on the other hand, similarly rejected Hinduism, not by proposing the existence of one god but by negating theism altogether, a position still held in Classical Buddhism.

You don't need a degree in mathematics to discern some fundamental contradictions here. If there are many gods, there cannot possibly be just one. If there is one god, there cannot possibly be many. If there is no god at all, there can neither be one god nor many. Hindus, Sikhs and Buddhists should, of course, learn to love and respect each other's humanity and freedom of expression, but they cannot for a moment—without sacrificing intellectual integrity—regard each other's 'theology' as *true* in any real sense of the word.

And if I, as an 'enlightened' Westerner, tried to convince these parties that in the end their faiths were one, would they not be justified in concluding that I was supremely arrogant? What unique insight into religious knowledge do I possess that enables me to relegate their fundamental propositions to the level of a minor theological variation on the same theme! I mean, the entire basis of Sikhism is that polytheism dishonours and detracts from the one true God. Who am I to insist that monotheism and polytheism really are 'one' after all?

Again, take the three great Middle Eastern faiths, Modern Judaism, Christianity and Islam. It is true that each of them affirms the existence of one Creator God, so in this sense they agree. But who are we to suggest that this shared proposition is the only important one? Central to the Christian faith is the conviction also that Jesus Christ was the Son of God (the promised Jewish Messiah) and that he died on a cross and rose again. This is non-negotiable for Christians—without it there is no Christianity. But modern Judaism insists that Jesus was not the Son of God but one of many pretenders to the title (Talmud: b. Sanhedrin 43a). The true Messiah, says Judaism, is yet to come. Logic alone forbids one from affirming at the same time that Jesus *is* and *is not* the Messiah. The Jew and the Christian can (and should) be friends but they cannot agree with each other's core beliefs.

The matter gets more complicated when we introduce Islam. The founding seventh-century A.D. Islamic prophet, Muhammad, venerated Jesus as a prophet but insisted that he neither died on a cross nor was the Son of God. Indeed, these Christian beliefs are described by the Koran as 'blasphemous' (Suras 4.157; 5.75-78). Thus, what is central to Christian faith is anathema in Islamic faith. The contradiction here is not small.

I was intrigued to read a *Sydney Morning Herald* article titled, 'The Love that Crosses the Great Divide'. The writer was at pains to demonstrate that "Jesus really is shared by both faiths". In a moment of unnoticed irony he argued that the Muslim Jesus is:

> not the Jesus who was the Son of God, admittedly, and who was crucified, but certainly the Jesus who was Messiah and miracle worker, who conversed regularly with God, who was born of a virgin and who ascended into heaven. (*Sydney Morning Herald*, 24 Dec 2001)

This latter picture of Jesus, the writer insisted, "crosses the great divide". At no point did the author seem aware that in the end all he was doing was advocating the Muslim Jesus over and above the Christian one.

For a Jesus who was not Son of God and who did not die on a cross is quite simply not the Jesus of Christian devotion. However noble the journalist's intentions, the article illustrated for me the futility of trying to argue for the essential sameness of the great faiths.

Many other contradictions could be explored: Christianity, for instance, insists that you are 'saved' by the grace and mercy of God, whereas Islam insists salvation is earned by ethical and ritual obedience; Judaism affirms that you enjoy just one life in this world (after which follows God's assessment), whereas Buddhism teaches a wheel of 'birth and re-birth' (similar to 'reincarnation') until you attain *Nirvana*, a state of blissful 'non-self'. You don't need to be a philosopher to work out that the differences here are profound.

English journalist and poet, Steve Turner, put the point well in the tongue-in-cheek poem, *Creed*:

> We believe that all religions are basically the same,
> at least the one that we read was.
> They all believe in love and goodness.
> They only differ on matters of
> creation sin heaven hell God and salvation.
> (Steve Turner, *Up To Date*, Hodder & Stoughton, London, 1993)

The faith-traditions of the world are in no sense *one*. Perhaps one or other is true, perhaps none is true, but it is simply not possible that all, or even a few, are true.

The mathematics of arrogance

Yet it is sometimes argued that to believe a particular religion is true (and therefore that others are untrue) is arrogant since, in doing so, you are consigning to error a huge portion of the rest of the world. "Those Christians are so arrogant," I occasionally hear, "how can they claim to have the truth when there are so many other paths?"

The argument is valid to a point—and let's face it, some Christians are arrogant—but if taken seriously it also produces a rather surprising conclusion. All opinions, by their very nature, consign others to error. Ironically, though, the views most open to the charge of arrogance are not the ancient monolithic ones such as Islam and Christianity, but the more recent ones like atheism and pluralism.

Let's start with atheism, the belief that there is no God or spiritual reality in the universe. This conviction is held by a tiny minority of the world's population: according to a review of numerous global studies on atheism, just 7% (Ariela Keysar and Juhem Navarro-Rivera, *The Oxford Handbook of Atheism*, 2015). That means that a mere 450 million people think that 93% of the world's six billion people are living by a false belief. This is quite a grandiose claim.

Islam, on the other hand, the second largest of the world's faiths, with approximately 1.5 billion adherents (or 22% of the world's population), consigns only 78% of the world's people to error. And Christianity, with 2.4 billion adherents (or 33% of the world's population), regards fewer still as mistaken.

In sheer numbers, then, Christianity may be regarded as the faith with the least pretentious claim to truth. Atheism, on the other hand, may be regarded as the faith with the most arrogant claim. 'Pluralism', the affirmation that all religions are essentially one, is likewise arrogant since it claims to know something about all the faiths that none of the individual faiths is able to perceive, namely, that behind the tensions there is an overarching truth which they all share.

I should be clear: I don't actually think this mathematical point is terribly significant. I'm simply pointing out the rather ironic upshot of the claim that it is arrogant to believe in one religious perspective over another.

I do not personally believe that strongly held views—even those that negate the views of others—are in themselves presumptuous or bigoted. They can certainly lead to arrogance, but they do not in themselves constitute an arrogant claim. To take just one example, if a Buddhist woman sincerely states her belief in Buddha's teaching about 'rebirth' after death—a belief which negates Islamic, Jewish and Christian teaching about the afterlife—is she behaving arrogantly? Surely not! In every other area of life—fashion, politics, history, science and so on—men and women have the freedom to think through a particular proposition and its attendant arguments and arrive at their own conclusion about the validity or otherwise of what is proposed. This is what our species, *Homo Sapiens* ('wise-man'), is about. Why on earth should this basic intellectual right be denied to people when it comes to as fundamental an area of human reflection as religion? It seems to me that to deny such a right in the name of cultural tolerance is both 'unwise' and, in itself, intolerant.

I suspect there are at least two reasons our society encourages openness to all religious claims and discourages the notion that any one of them may be true or false. I don't think it has only to do with sounding sophisticated at parties: "Oh yes I've always felt that the various religions embrace one essential reality!"

The myth of tolerance

The first reason is the one I have already hinted at: the fear that religious conviction will lead to religious intolerance and, as a consequence, to discrimination and violence. As I said earlier, the fear is understandable. History is full of examples of violent intolerance on the part of those claiming Christian, Islamic, Buddhist, Jewish or Hindu justifications.

It was precisely this bloody history of cultural and religious intolerance that led to the UN General Assembly's declaration in 1993 that 1995 should be hailed the "International Year for Tolerance". The year was marked by hundreds of cultural events and conferences designed to promote tolerance. Tragically, the Year of Tolerance failed to head off some of the most gruesome examples of fundamentalist extremism and sectarian violence ever witnessed—the Balkans, September 11, Palestine, just to name a few.

Our aversion to religious intolerance is perfectly

reasonable. But is an acceptance of all religious truth-claims the best way to respond to such dangers? I, for one, do not think so. A better way forward, I believe, is to promote true 'tolerance', a word often used but rarely, if ever, defined.

Tolerance in our modern usage has come to mean simply a willingness to accept as valid another person's point of view. For a Muslim, then, modern-day 'tolerance' would mean a willingness to accept as valid the Buddhist teaching that, contrary to the *Koran*, human beings experience many lives, not just one. Alternatively, for a Buddhist, modern-day 'tolerance' would mean a willingness to accept as valid the Islamic teaching, in contrast to the words of Buddha, that after just one life a person faces the judgement of God. Can such acceptance really be understood as tolerance? The answer has to be 'no'.

By definition, tolerance must involve an awareness of something contrary—the word comes from the Latin 'tolerare', meaning *to endure* opposition. True tolerance, then, is not my willingness to accept the position of another; it is the more admirable ability to treat with respect a person with whom I deeply disagree. A tolerant Muslim, for instance, is not one who accepts as valid the Buddhist doctrine of 'birth and rebirth', it is one who, while rejecting such a teaching, is able to remain respectful and compassionate toward Buddhists themselves. Again, the tolerant Christian is not one who accepts as valid the Hindu claim that there are many gods; it is the one who, while denying polytheism, is able to treat Hindus with the honour due to them as fellow members of the human race. In each case there is both an informed awareness of the contrary position of the other and a generous commitment to respect and value the person who holds that position.

By contrast, our common insistence upon mere 'agreement' is intellectually suspect and culturally insensitive. Moreover, it tends to mute healthy discussion and debate among the faiths and so, ironically, has the potential in fact to fuel suspicion and speculation about the 'other'. This is a recipe for bigotry and intolerance.

True tolerance, on the other hand, is both intellectually rigorous and culturally sensitive, in that it acknowledges the real differences among the faiths. Perhaps more importantly, it has the power to dispel bigotry and discrimination based on differences. For if we could all learn to honour and care for those with whom we profoundly disagree, our disagreements would only ever provide the basis for engagement and discussion with others, never fear and hostility toward them. We would be free to contradict but never to disrespect, to persuade but never to coerce. In a multicultural society like ours, tolerance of this kind is a rare and greatly needed commodity.

Economy of effort

But there is probably a second reason our society encourages openness to all religious claims. It has to do not with the noble desire for getting along with each other but with the long-held Western tradition of choosing the easier of two options. Some might call it 'apathy'; I prefer to call it 'economy of effort'.

Suppose you were to ask two Chinese friends how to say *'I love you'* in Mandarin. One of them promptly replies: "That's simple: *'Wo ai ni'.*" Immediately, the other friend retorts: "No, no, it is pronounced: *'Wo hen ni'.*" You now have a problem which can be resolved in one of two ways. On the one hand, you could research the issue. This might involve finding another Chinese friend and asking for clarification, or perhaps going to the local library and looking up the entry in the *English-Mandarin Dictionary*. It might take a little effort but at least in the end you could make an informed decision.

The other option is far easier. Rather than dwell on the discrepancy in their replies, you could simply assume that each of their answers was essentially correct: perhaps they were just different ways of saying the same thing; perhaps they were dialect variations of one original expression. After all there was only a one syllable difference in the answers: how divergent could they be! Affirming both answers as true, then, will both avoid upsetting anyone and require no effort on your part whatsoever. It's the perfect economy of effort, except that, in reality, "Wo hen ni" means 'I hate you'!

I'm sure you can see my point. When a Hindu affirms the existence of many gods and a Jew the existence of just one, it produces a dilemma which can be resolved in one of two ways. On the one hand, you could investigate for yourself the historical and philosophical justifications for polytheism versus monotheism. This might involve reading a book or two on the subject or perhaps just getting alone and thinking the issue through. Alternatively, you could take the simpler option and affirm both claims as valid in their own way. After all, perhaps 'the many' are just portions of 'the one' or something like that.

To take another example, when a Christian affirms Jesus' death on the cross and a Muslim refutes the same, what do you do? You could look into it yourself checking what historians reckon happened to Jesus. But far easier would be to accept both claims as true in their own way. While this would require a degree of 'mental elasticity'—since, in reality, he either did or did not die by crucifixion—it is clearly the option requiring less effort.

In short, I am suggesting that our society's keenness to affirm all religious views stems, in part, from an aversion to having to think too hard about any of them. To decide between the Islamic doctrine of salvation by human obedience and the Christian doctrine of salvation by God's free grace might involve comparing the respective Scriptures and pondering whether, in your view, human beings could meet the Maker's standards. Choosing between the Buddhist doctrine of 'rebirth' and the Jewish insistence on a single life might involve investigating the respective rationale for each belief or, perhaps, evaluating the credibility of modern past-lives claims. Far easier to remain blissfully 'open' to all of it.

I'm sure this isn't true of all Westerners—the fact that you are reading this book is evidence of that—but it is difficult to resist the conclusion that something like 'economy of effort' has influenced our talk about spirituality.

And the result of all this is rather sad. Whether by an aversion to religious intolerance or a tendency to take the easy option, this acceptance of all faiths has the potential to leave us without faith at all. God, whoever he or she is, remains for us a mystery. We, like the ancient Athenians, are left with altars, at least in our hearts, to an 'unknown god'.

But surely if there were a spiritual reality intended for us all, we should expect some tangible signpost in the world pointing us in the right direction. Surely God would not leave his creatures with nothing but a bewildering variety of religious voices to gain our attention. Would not the Almighty—if indeed he exists—have made things decidedly clearer?

The Apostle Paul, in his speech to the speculative Athenians, answered with a resounding 'yes'. And the subject of his answer back then provides the basis of faith today for one-third of the world's population. It is to this subject that we turn in the final chapters, as we explore one critical distinction between the claims of the world's major religions and those of Christianity. It is the issue of 'verifiability'—a mouthful of a word but one which, when understood in relation to faith, makes a world of difference.

4

God's signpost

Dreams and visions

Imagine for a moment that a friend came to you today with the unusual claim that last night his great, great grandmother appeared to him in a dream offering insights into the nature of the spiritual realm and of the best path to reach true spirituality. These insights included detailed descriptions of the afterlife, advice on which foods to avoid and a collection of prayers that ought to be said in order to attain enlightenment. Imagine further that your friend wrote down in a notebook all that he could remember of the matriarch's words. He now asks you to read the notes and consider embracing this new spiritual perspective for yourself.

Suppose now that another friend came to you tomorrow with the equally unusual claim that her great, great-grandfather appeared to her in a dream offering her insights into spiritual reality. These insights were radically different from the ones recounted by your other friend. The afterlife was repudiated, all foods were deemed edible and mantras, not prayers, were promised to hold the key to spiritual truth. This friend also wrote down the contents of the dream and asks you now to consider her revelations as the new path for your life.

You now have a problem, and I don't just mean having to find some new friends! Leaving aside the bizarre nature of the revelations, the situation proposed here highlights a critical question which presents itself to all religious claims: *how can the truth or falsehood of one's claim be tested?*

The contradictions between the two 'revelations' would indicate that both could not be true, but how could you test which—if, indeed, either—were actually true? Quite simply, you could not. The character of the revelations means that they are beyond the scope of human enquiry. Of course, you could subject your friends to lie-detector tests but this would demonstrate only whether or not the claims were made up. Even if both claimants could be shown not to have lied, this does nothing to indicate the truthfulness or otherwise of the content of the dreams. Dreams and visions are, by their very nature, imperceptible to all but the visionaries themselves.

A world of 'unverifiable' claims

Philosophically speaking, claims such as these may be deemed 'unverifiable'. 'Unverifiable' does not mean *untrue*, it simply means that a thing can't be tested one way or the other. They are beyond scientific or historical scrutiny.

Virtually all of the world's religions are at their

core unverifiable. Again, this is not for a moment to say that they are untrue, only that they cannot be verified one way or the other. Indeed, the two examples just offered provide quite a close analogy to the nature and content (though not the significance) of the world's major religious claims.

Buddhism, for instance, rests entirely on the insights gained by Siddhartha Gautama, the sixth-century B.C. Indian prince. After seven years of ascetic denial and contemplation the young prince finally received his 'enlightenment' (Buddha means 'enlightened one') while meditating under a Bo Tree one night in May. The Buddha's enlightenment consisted of insights into the true goal of life (the negation of self and desire), the nature of the afterlife (*karma* and 'rebirth') and various ethical and culinary disciplines required of those wishing to gain enlightenment. Neither the fact nor the content of that enlightenment can be tested. Nevertheless, the Buddha soon gathered around him a small group of devoted disciples who with him began to promote these teachings throughout the land. The teachings were then compiled in *The Dhammapada* or the *Sayings of the Buddha*, the most cherished Scriptures of *Theravada* (or 'classical') Buddhism.

Islam is likewise grounded in a revelation of a private and mystical nature, the content of which is beyond analysis. Muhammad, a seventh-century A.D. nobleman from Arabia was from childhood inclined to ponder matters religious. One day in 610, however, his private reflections were enhanced by an angelic vision announcing to him: "You are the Messenger of God." From this time until his death in 632 Muhammad received frequent and very detailed revelations. Although these revelations are said to have been accompanied occasionally by sounds (such as a bell), the messages themselves were perceived only in the Prophet's heart. The content of these communications varied, sometimes disclosing ethical and ritual demands, sometimes listing 'corrections' of Jewish and Christian teachings, and sometimes expounding purely doctrinal themes. All of these were subsequently proclaimed by Muhammad, committed to memory by his disciples and compiled in the Islamic holy book, the *Koran*.

The point of the above précis is not to criticize Buddhism and Islam but merely to highlight the essentially unverifiable premise of their claims. Let me reiterate, this is not the same as saying these faiths are untrue. I am simply drawing attention to the nature of their claims. Even if we assume Siddhartha and Muhammad did not make up their stories (a fairly reasonable assumption in my opinion) this tells us nothing about the truthfulness or otherwise of the content of their revelations. To recall the opening examples, a lie-detector might show that your visionary friend was not lying but it will not be able to validate the content of the vision itself. Such a revelation is, by its very nature, beyond verification.

Without turning this book into a study in comparative religion, let me state quite simply that most of the world's religious claims are similarly unverifiable (though, again, not therefore false). Confucianism, Hinduism, Sikhism, Baha'i and Shintoism all share this basic premise.

For the faithful of such religions the unverifiable nature of their beliefs actually provides something of a shelter from the arguments of critics. For no matter what humanity discovers about the physical universe or the events of history, claims such as these will remain untouched. The belief that Allah requires five times of prayer a day cannot be disproved. The claim that life's goal is the removal of desire via the Buddha's Eightfold Path cannot be shown to be false. Neither of these beliefs may take your fancy, but nor could you demonstrate them to be untrue. The Muslim, the Buddhist, the Hindu, the Sikh and so on, all live in the security that their faith is unassailable. It is unprovable, yes! It is a matter of pure faith, yes! But with this unverifiability comes an invincibility not enjoyed by those few traditions which dare to make verifiable claims.

Let me now turn to this handful of traditions.

In search of a signpost

To recall the hypotheticals earlier in the chapter, let me offer an example of a verifiable claim.

Imagine a friend came to you today with the unusual claim that last night his great, great grandmother appeared to him offering new insights into the spiritual realm. This time, however, the revelation came not in the form of a private dream or vision but in that of a giant apparition in the middle of Oxford Street, London. In fact, the matriarch's appearing, it was claimed, was so public it stopped peak hour traffic for two hours. Several hundred pedestrians and drivers stood dumbfounded as she explained that her visitation was a kind of signpost from God designed to point the residents of London in the direction of spiritual truth. Being closest to the old lady, your friend took furious notes and later interviewed other eye-witnesses to gain their perspectives. These insights were then compiled in a notebook and offered to you for your consideration.

Again, leaving aside the bizarre content of this 'revelation', the claim itself is a 'verifiable' one. The truth or falsehood of the claim can, to a degree, be tested. You could listen to news reports and see if the alleged event rated a mention; you could do an analysis of the scene itself to see if incidental details in the witness reports matched up; you could assess the traffic congestion reports of the police; you could perhaps even do background checks on the witnesses to see if their testimonies were reliable. You may not be able to prove the event beyond all doubt but you could certainly arrive at a reasonable conclusion regarding the credibility or otherwise of the claim.

A claim such as this is verifiable. 'Verifiable' does not mean true—just as unverifiable does not mean untrue—it simply means that a thing can be tested. It is open to scientific or historical scrutiny. It may be, for instance, that after investigating the scene in Oxford Street and interviewing various witnesses, you conclude that your friend's claim is false. Perhaps witnesses' recollections were too hazy to be of use or so precisely similar as to arouse your suspicion. Perhaps the claim of a two-hour traffic jam found no support in either the police records or the public transport logs. This being the case, your friend's verifiable claim may be verified as improbable and, therefore, as not warranting your devotion.

The title of this book reflects a sentiment not of my own invention but one which arises regularly in conversations with people who wouldn't normally call themselves 'religious'. They say something to this effect: "If the Creator of the universe were the least bit interested in our devotion, he or she would surely do something 'concrete' to grab our attention, something we could all assess for ourselves and from which we could draw our own conclusions. Surely, he would make himself clearer!"

I find the sentiment compelling—obviously so since I have written a book about it. It just does not seem reasonable that the Almighty—if indeed the Almighty exists—would have left the world without a signpost to his presence, without some tangible moment on the world stage which turned the 'unknown God' into the known one. In other words, my hunch is that if there is a spiritual reality to which we are all invited, claims about that reality would be of a verifiable nature, not an unverifiable one.

Otherwise we would be left in the dilemma spoken of throughout the book, the dilemma the ancient Athenians found themselves in—an openness to a host of divinities which results in the admission of God's final 'unknowability'.

So, of course, the question is: which religions are premised on verifiable claims, claims which can be investigated and found to be either credible or *in*credible? There are I think three: Judaism, Christianity and Mormonism.

The Book of Mormon

Let me begin with Mormonism because this provides an example of a verifiable claim which, in my opinion, can be found (with a high degree of confidence) to be unwarranted.

Joseph Smith, the founder of Mormonism (or more correctly, The Church of Jesus Christ of Latter-Day Saints), grew up in New York in the early 1800s, a time of great religious revivalism. In 1827, at the age of 22, Smith claimed that an angelic being had led him to buried golden plates. Upon these plates was inscribed a 'history' of the American Indians who, according to the account, were really descendants of the ancient Hebrews who had emigrated from Palestine to North America centuries before Christ— though Christ was said to have visited these American tribes soon after his resurrection. Smith translated the plates with the aid of special reading lenses made of diamond and published his work under the title *The Book of Mormon*, named after the ancient prophet who was said to have originally inscribed the plates.

At one level Joseph Smith's claim is unverifiable. No one else met the angelic being and Smith alone was able to translate the plates (from a supposed dialect of Egyptian). However, because the *Book of Mormon* is essentially historical in its claims it is, to a high degree, open to historical and archaeological scrutiny (in a way not possible in the 1800s).

To begin with, not one example of 'Reformed Egyptian' (the language in which the golden plates were supposedly written) has been uncovered by any archaeologist or Egyptologist anywhere in the world. Moreover, the cities, tribes, battles and practices described in the *Book of Mormon* find no support in the extensive archaeological data relating to the history of North America now available. The claim, furthermore, that native Americans descend from Hebrews has been undermined by modern anthropological studies which trace the ancestry of Native Americans through East-Asian Mongoloids (not Semites) who migrated from Asia 20,000-35,000 years ago.

In short, what the *Book of Mormon* claims to have taken place in North America between 600 B.C.-400 A.D. appears simply not to have happened. The claims are looked upon with suspicion even by as even-handed a source as the *Encyclopaedia Britannica*:

> Most non-Mormon scholars, however, regard the book as a collection of local legends of Indian origin, fragments of autobiography, and current religious and political controversies... all transformed with remarkable ingenuity into a religious document. (2001 CD-ROM edition)

In other words, while the *Book of Mormon* may, in a sheer act of faith, be accepted as true by the world's ten million Mormons, the claims contained in it do not inspire confidence for the enquiring outsider. A tangible signpost of God's dealings in the world does not appear to be present in the Mormon faith.

What then of Judaism and Christianity, religions premised on equally verifiable claims?

The Jewish 'exit'

The Jewish Scriptures, known as the Torah (corresponding to the Christian 'Old Testament'), contain numerous ethical laws, prophecies and theological pronouncements. However, the basis of the book, the thing upon which everything else rests, is an event said to have occurred 1200 years or so before Christ. The Jewish people, who had for years been a slave nation under the Pharaohs of Egypt, are said to have miraculously escaped the clutches of Rameses II and travelled to modern Palestine (i.e. Canaan or the 'promised land') where they settled and became the nation of Israel. This 'exodus' (exit), as it is called, was intended to demonstrate for Jew and Gentile alike God's intention to involve himself with the world through the Jewish people: it was God's signpost.

In broad terms, historical investigation into the exodus produces some interesting results. The names and places recounted in the biblical narrative correspond with what we know of Egyptian culture at just this time. This at least implies that the exodus story arose out of an Egyptian context, not a later Jewish one. Moreover, Egyptian records place Semitic peoples (of whom the Jews were one) in Egyptian slavery at the time, and the building works said in the Bible to have been the focus of the Israelites' slave-labour, the cities of Pithon and Rameses, were indeed built by Rameses II at this time.

In addition, although Egyptian annals make no mention of a Jewish exodus—Pharaohs tended to record only victories over their subjects—one hieroglyph from about 50 years later does place the Israelites not down in Egypt but up in Canaan instead. This corresponds well with the time the biblical record has the Jews occupying that territory.

Please be clear: my point here is not that the exodus, and therefore Judaism, can be proven. I am simply underlining the fact that at its heart, and by its very nature, Judaism is one of only three religions premised on verifiable claims. And, unlike Mormonism, when scrutinized, the claims of Judaism arouse not suspicion but a degree of confidence.

But what of Christianity?

Jesus Christ and Judaism

The first thing to say in order correctly to understand the faith of one third of the world is that Christianity did not arise as a counter-movement against another. As stated earlier, Buddhism and Sikhism originated as off-shoots and rejections of Hinduism. In the same way, Islam and Baha'i were counter-movements to prior traditions: Islam to Judaism and Christianity, and Baha'i to (Shi'ite) Islam.

Not so with Christianity. It probably goes without saying that Jesus and his apostles and most of the earliest believers were all devout Jews. In no sense was the early movement surrounding Jesus a rejection of Judaism. Rather, it was proclaimed throughout the Mediterranean as the very fulfillment of the Jewish Scriptures. The Torah, written centuries before Jesus, promised a number of things about the coming kingly Messiah: that he would be a descendant of king David (2 Samuel 7:4-17); that he would be born in Bethlehem in the South (Micah 5:2) and emerge from Galilee in the North (Isaiah 9:1-7); that he would rule by the power of his teaching not the sword (Isaiah 11:1-10); and, finally, that he would die as an atonement for the wrongs of the world before rising again to life (Isaiah 52:13–53:12). It was the presence in the Torah of prophecies such as these that led, in part, to the early successes of infant Christianity. Christianity (as we now call it) was seen in its beginning as a Jewish renewal movement.

The later Jewish leadership eventually rejected

Jesus as Messiah, demanding that the followers of Jesus be excommunicated from the synagogues and regarded as blasphemers (this took place shortly before A.D. 100 during the councils of Jamnia, a city near the coast of Southern Palestine). Why this took place is a very complex question, but it largely had to do with Jesus' *non*-fulfilment of the militaristic hopes of first-century Jews. Many Jews hoped for a Messiah who would destroy the occupying forces of Rome and establish the kingdom of God on earth. But Jesus went around saying odd things like 'turn the other cheek', 'love your enemies' and 'the meek will inherit the earth'. In any case, my point here is that Christians did not reject Judaism; the Jewish leadership rejected Jesus as their Messiah.

Hence, when I come to speak of the claims of Christianity I am not setting them against the claims of biblical Judaism. From the Christian point of view, Christianity only affirms ancient Judaism. Modern Jews may wish to set their beliefs against those of Christians but this is not because of anything in the Jewish Scriptures themselves—how could it be, since the Torah was completed centuries before Jesus?—it is rather the result of a tradition codified at Jamnia and practised ever since. One may even say that the Christian feels no need to establish the validity of biblical Judaism since Christianity takes for granted that Judaism is true. Establishing the Christian claim automatically establishes the ancient Jewish one. Or, to put it more tongue-in-cheekily, verifying the truth of

Christianity kills two historical birds with one 'rolled-away' stone!

So, what is the claim of Christianity and in what way is it verifiable?

Jesus Christ and God

The problem raised throughout this book is the apparent unknowability of God. While it is attractive to think that all religions point us to God, the reality is they do not. The contradictions inherent among the various faiths make clear that a degree of speculation is at work behind many of the faiths and perhaps behind all of them. Where may clarity be found?

The unique answer to this question posed by Christianity is both bizarre and intriguing. God, affirms the Christian tradition, has quelled the need for spiritual speculation by offering the world an historical revelation of himself in the person of Jesus Christ. Perhaps a well-used illustration can highlight the significance of this claim.

Imagine, if you will, what my wife looks like. By now, you've read several thousand of my words; you could perhaps begin to construct an image of the sort of girl I would be attracted to or, more perplexing, what sort of girl would be attracted to me! Suppose now you were to draw a sketch of my wife as she appears in your mind and send it to me for review.

Even if a thousand readers took part in this odd experiment (please don't!), the chances of any one of the sketches accurately portraying my wife are pretty slender. Some of the drawings might be beautiful—even more beautiful than the real thing! Others may be works of great intelligence or artistry, the sort of thing that, while not accurate, would still be worthy of our admiration. In the end, however, unless one of you had met my wife, the sketches would all be guesses. A beautiful, intelligent and artistic guess is still a guess.

Turn now, if you will, to the top left corner of page 80 and there you will find a small photo of the beauty in question.

I placed the photo there not just to satisfy your curiosity or for you to check your accuracy but to illustrate something unique about the Christian claim. Jesus is to God what that photo is to my wife: a revelation to end the speculation.

When asked by one of his disciples, "Lord, show us (God) the Father," Jesus replied, "Have I been with you so long, and you still do not know me, Philip? Whoever has seen me has seen the Father" (John 14:8-9). If true, this means that when we see Jesus thundering in debate against religious hypocrites or tenderly offering forgiveness to 'sinners', we see God. It means that when we see Jesus humbly accept ridicule and bravely endure death on a cross, we see God.

This is an astonishing claim. Siddhartha Gautama never said this; Guru Nanak never said this; Muhammad would never have dreamed of saying this. Jesus alone claimed personally to reveal God not through a mystical dream or a divine dictation but through what he was, what he said and what he did. The religions of the world may be artistic expressions of our spiritual hunches but if God has left a tangible photo of himself on the world stage, their significance as signposts to the truth is greatly diminished. We are left wondering if they are not in the end creative guesses.

Jesus Christ and history

But what marks out this Christian claim as worthy of one's confidence? In what way was is it different from, say, the claim of Muhammad that the words he heard in his heart were the very words of God? To answer this I can do no better than to return to Paul's speech to the Athenian intellectuals.

Having argued that human cultures are wired for contact with God, and having drawn attention to the Athenians' own admission (implicit in the presence of an altar to an 'unknown God') that God remains for them 'unknown', Paul proceeds to emphasize the verifiable nature of the Christian claim:

> "The times of ignorance God overlooked, but now he commands all people everywhere to repent, because he has fixed a day on which he will judge the world in righteousness by a man [*the Messiah Jesus*] whom he has appointed; and of this he has given assurance to all by raising him from the dead." (ACTS 17:30-31)

The news of Christ—his life, death and resurrection—
is not mythical narrative revealed in the head of a
prophet and transcribed in books called Gospels. It was
a phenomenon of time and space; it was an event of
history. At its heart, Christianity concerns the public,
verifiable life story of the man Jesus, the man who
claimed personally to reveal God and of whom God
has 'given assurance', to use Paul's words, by raising
him from the dead.

Philosophically, this claim belongs to a different
category entirely from that of Hinduism, Buddhism,
Sikhism, Islam, and Baha'i. Paul's news concerned not
simply timeless spiritual truths, but actual events which
occurred just recently over the other side of the
Mediterranean—events about a man who forgave pros-
titutes, rebuked religious bigots, healed the sick, died
for sins and, most importantly, rose from the dead. This
constitutes a verifiable claim, a *daringly* verifiable one.

The head on the block

Before I attempt, in the broadest way, to outline the
key lines of verification for the Christian claim, let me
stop and explain what I mean by the '*daringly* verifiable' nature of Christianity.

I stated earlier that unverifiable truth-claims enjoy
a measure of invincibility from the arguments of critics. At one level, this must be a source of comfort for
adherents. For regardless of what scientists and historians discover about the world, the claims of such

faiths will remain unchallenged.

By contrast, the historical and event-centred nature of the Christian claim leaves it awkwardly vulnerable to the examination of critics. It is as if Christianity deliberately places its neck on the proverbial chopping block of public scrutiny, and invites anyone who wishes to take a swing. And 'swing' they do. Scientists analyze the ancient papyri documents of Jesus' biographies (the Gospels) to assess their age and reliability; archaeologists dig up sections of Galilee to see if Jesus' stomping ground has been accurately described by the New Testament writers; historians pore over the literary and inscriptional evidence from non-Christian sources to see if place names, personal titles and architectural details can be confirmed, and if any of Jesus' activities rated a mention outside the writings of the faithful. Moreover, they scrutinize the New Testament documents themselves to see if there are enough signs of independent testimony surrounding the events of Jesus to warrant confidence in what they claim.

This vulnerability to scrutiny makes some Christians nervous. They live with the thought that just around the corner there may be some new discovery that will undermine their faith.

The recent controversy over the Dead Sea Scrolls provides an interesting example. Since the scrolls were discovered in 1947 there has been no end of rumours and innuendo about how the scrolls have been kept from the public eye because of the damaging evidence they supposedly offer against the traditional understanding of Jesus' life. Controversial books were written, startling documentaries were shown on TV, and 'earth-shattering' articles appeared in *Time* magazine. However, now that all the swings have been taken and the dust has settled, the international academic community is calling for restraint. For not only are the scrolls readily available (in both their original languages and in English) but, it turns out, the consensus of scholarship dates the relevant scrolls to the period just before Jesus. Hence, while the scrolls provide excellent background information about some forms of Judaism in the pre-Christian era, they have nothing directly to say about Jesus himself. What was touted as damaging for Christianity a few years ago has proven only to clarify and confirm the picture of ancient Judaism we already find in the New Testament.

Many, many other examples could be offered. My aim here, though, is not to rebut recent criticisms of Christianity but merely to illustrate something of the nature of the Christian faith: Christianity is potentially vulnerable to critical enquiry precisely because its main claims are verifiable. This is perhaps a cause for fear among some believers but the reality is, for every scholarly criticism throughout the years there have been dozens of equally scholarly responses. And as the dust settles and nervous Christians begin to breathe again, the immense Christian claim simply lifts up its gaze to the crowd, places its head on the chopping block once more, and invites the next person to take a swing.

It is telling also that throughout all these controversies large numbers of first rate scholars from all of the relevant disciplines—history, archaeology, science, literary criticism, as well as from theology—have professed faith in the 'daringly verifiable' claims about Jesus. It is true that many other academics are Buddhists, Muslims and Hindus as well. This, however, is not so significant since the claims of these faiths are untouched by the scrutiny of these disciplines. The fact that Christianity is so potentially vulnerable to scholarship and yet is still believed by so many professional scholars is not without significance.

The openness of Christianity to rigorous scrutiny is, in my opinion, one of the most exciting things about it. I want a faith that can be tested. I can appreciate how Muslims, Buddhists and Hindus would find security in the knowledge that their beliefs can never be disproved. But, for me, this would never satisfy. I don't think I could shake off the feeling that if God were truly interested in our attention he would offer more than a dream, a vision or a personal dictation of divine words; he would surely present some tangible, verifiable signpost to himself. The fact that Christianity claims to do just this, combined with the fact that the more this claim is scrutinized the more substantial it appears, makes me anything but nervous. It thrills me.

5

Lines of verification

A thorough presentation of the evidence for Christ would require several lengthy books, and scholars vastly more qualified than I am have already filled the shelves of the libraries of the world with such works. For the titles of some of the important ones, see the list at the back of the book on page 81.

Let me make clear, though, that my aim here is not to 'prove' the Christian claim at all. My hope is far more modest. By outlining the main lines of verification open to the interested enquirer I want simply to *illustrate* the broadly verifiable nature of Christianity. What follows then is not designed to convince the reader of the truth of Christianity—personally, I doubt many people decide to follow Christ merely through the presentation of 'evidence' anyway. Rather, it is intended to demonstrate that of all the great religious claims in the world, the Christian one is the most easily and widely testable. What I'm saying is that if God *has* left the world with a tangible signpost of his presence, the one said to be found in Christianity provides interested enquirers with a worthy place from which to begin the search. That, in a sentence, is what this book is all about.

With this stated aim out in the open, let me outline just four common lines of verification for the claims about Jesus Christ.

The quality of the documentary evidence

The first line of evidence has to do with the quality of the documentary evidence. Four things can be said about this.

First, the language of these documents is not some strange tongue which no one understands any more. It is called *Koine Greek* and it is a very simple and widely understood language. One can be totally confident that what one reads in a modern English translation of the Gospels today is a direct and accurate rendering of what was written in the first century.

Secondly, the age of the documentary evidence is impressive. For writings as ancient as these, scholars never expect to find the original document itself. Rather, they hope to find copies that are as close as possible to the date of the original. So, for instance, the oldest available manuscript of the works of Plato (who died in 347 B.C.) is a copy made in 895 A.D. That's a gap of more than one thousand years. Nevertheless, because ancient copying techniques were on the whole so precise, historians have few qualms relying on such a document as an accurate copy of the original. By comparison, the earliest manuscript copies of the Gospels are dated around 200 A.D., only 120 years or so after they were first written.

Thirdly, the volume of copies we possess is overwhelming. For the writings of Plato, Aristotle, Julius Caesar, Tacitus and other ancient giants, we possess only a handful of separate manuscripts. As exaggerated as it sounds, for the Gospels alone (not including the rest of the New Testament) historians have approximately 2000 manuscript copies with which to work.

Fourthly, the stability of the copying process is very clear. Because we can compare copies of the Gospels produced, say, in 600 A.D. with those copied in 200 A.D. we are able to confirm the high accuracy of the copying process. Historians in the field have no problem conceding that what was originally penned has been carefully preserved. To quote the *Encyclopaedia Britannica* again: "Compared with other ancient manuscripts, the text of the New Testament is dependable and consistent".

Confirmation of non-Christian sources

In case anyone should think that the life of Jesus is simply a well documented fairytale, the second line of evidence makes clear that it is not.

The broad outline of Jesus' life is confirmed by several passing references to him in non-Christian writings of the period: three from Roman authors (once each in Tacitus, Suetonius and Pliny) and four from Jewish pens (twice each in Josephus and the Talmud). If one pieces together all the information contained in these statements, one learns when Jesus lived, where he lived, that his mother was named Mary and that his conception was irregular, that he was a renowned teacher, that he did things which both friends and foes thought to be supernatural, that he was given the title Messiah, that he was executed, how, and by whom, that he had a brother who was also executed, that people claimed he was raised from the dead, and that his followers continued to worship and proclaim him after he was gone. All this without opening a Bible.

The integrity of the Gospel accounts

So, when we turn to the third line of evidence, the Gospels themselves, we can be confident that in broad terms they are good historical sources.

Several things add to our picture of the integrity of the Gospels. First is the date they were composed. I mentioned earlier that the manuscript copies of the Gospels we possess are quite close to the time when the original was penned. But equally impressive is the fact that the original time of writing was very close to the time of the events themselves. The first Gospel was probably written in the mid-60s A.D., just 30 or so years after Jesus' death. All of the Gospels were written within 50 years of his death. For ancient history this is about as good as it gets. Tacitus, for instance, the greatest of Rome's historians, wrote his account of Emperor Augustus' reign over 100 years after the emperor's death. But even this poses little problem for the historian since we know that such works were not composed out of thin air but relied on existing sources dating back closer to the events.

Secondly, to write any work of history (ancient or modern) an author uses various sources, whether eyewitness testimonies, log books, court records, or previously written histories. The same is true of the Gospel writers. Most New Testament scholars discern behind the Gospels at least five separate sources, each composed prior to the Gospels themselves. When these sources are independently analyzed (quite a precarious task and something of an obsession among some) the picture of Jesus which emerges from these is strikingly similar across the sources: independently of each other they describe a teacher, a healer and one known as the promised Messiah who died and rose again. When independent sources say basically the same thing about an event or person of history, it's a good indication of historical reliability.

Thirdly, the incidental historical accuracy of the Gospels is also important. When the Gospels say something in passing about, say, the architecture or politics of a town Jesus visited, we can quite often confirm these details by modern archaeological and literary analysis. A classic example is the story in John 5 where mention is made of a bathing pool Jesus visited in Jerusalem which, according to John, had five rows of columns. Because archaeologists had dug up all over Jerusalem without finding such pool, there was initially some scholarly doubt cast over the accuracy of John's Gospel. Then, as digs progressed, a pool was found in the North-East quarter of the old city and the remains of five colonnades could still be seen. Many, many other such examples are available to the interested enquirer.

The resurrection of Jesus Christ

The fourth line of evidence is, to my mind, the most compelling: the resurrection of Christ. Indeed, this was the climactic statement of Paul's speech: "God", he said, "has given proof of this to all men by raising him from the dead."

The resurrection of Christ is the event by which Christianity stands or falls. It is the 'assurance', as Paul says, that this man is God's appointed judge and king over the world. This is *the* divine signpost, says Christianity, the proverbial 'X-marks-the-spot' for God's activity on the world stage. The resurrection of Christ is God's proof and pledge that, in Jesus, salvation from divine judgement is secured, satisfaction for the soul may be enjoyed, and eternal life (our own 'resurrection', if you like) is assured.

The Washington based world news service, United Press International (UPI), reported:

> In a dramatic turnaround from post-Enlightenment skepticism, historians are now inclined to give much more credence to the New Testament accounts of the Resurrection than their predecessors. (Uwe Siemon-Netto,

'Historians Say Resurrection a Reality', United
Press International, 11 April 2001)

So what is this new-found scholarly 'credence' based on?
What 'lines of verification' relate to the resurrection?
I will mention just five, although if you have the time to
explore some of the books on the reading list you will
find that there are many more.

First, there is the claim itself. This may sound
strange at first but in any historical or legal argument,
one of the first pieces of evidence to consider is always
the testimony concerning the events in question. That
numerous apparently sane people claimed to have seen
Jesus risen from the dead is a fact of history. And it's a
fact that requires an explanation. It may be that after
all the other facts have been heard one will discredit
the claim, but the claim itself must be admitted
provisionally as evidence.

Secondly, there is the empty tomb. Historians
working in the field will generally concede the veracity
of the empty tomb of Jesus. There seems to be no
other explanation for why, when the apostles began to
proclaim Jesus' resurrection in the city of Jerusalem
itself, the body of Jesus was never produced to counter
the claim. It was not as if opponents could not have
found the tomb; it belonged to one of Jerusalem's elite
politicians, Joseph of Arimathea. Furthermore, we
know from two separate sources from the period that
the Jewish leadership conceded the empty tomb. They
just raised questions about how it got that way.

Thirdly, according to all four Gospels, the first witnesses to the resurrection were women. This does not sound significant until one realizes that in this period a woman's testimony was regarded as spurious and carried little legal weight. Hence, if one were making up a story about a resurrection and wanting fellow Jews to believe it, one would not include women as the initial witnesses, unless of course it just happened to be (embarrassingly) true.

Fourthly, the slight but significant divergence in the various accounts of the resurrection supports their credibility. Like police assessing the evidence of witnesses, historians look not only for general agreement between various accounts of a particular event ('convergence') but also for small individual variations ('divergence'). The few divergences tell you the witnesses have not simply copied each other's stories. The Gospels certainly fare well in the quest for a level of convergence/divergence.

Fifthly, perhaps the most compelling line of verification for the resurrection of Jesus is the transformation of Jesus' followers. How is it that a group of several hundred Jewish 'nobodies' came, not only to believe they'd seen Jesus raised from the dead, but to announce this fact widely and tenaciously all the way to trials, torture and, for many, death? It is one thing to die for an ideology you simply believe to be true—plenty of people have done this—but it is another thing entirely to die for a claim you, as an alleged eyewitness, know to be a lie. So compelling is this transformation of Jesus' followers that a leading German historian (now passed away), Dr. Pinchas Lapide, writes:

> How was it possible that his disciples, who by no means excelled in intelligence, eloquence, or strength of faith, were able to begin their victorious march of conversion?... In a purely logical analysis, the resurrection of Jesus is 'the lesser of two evils' for all those who seek a rational explanation of the worldwide consequences of that Easter faith. Thus according to my opinion, the resurrection belongs to the category of the truly real. (*The Resurrection of Jesus: a Jewish perspective*, SPCK, London, 1984)

I should add that Professor Lapide was a Jewish historian, not a Christian believer, and the rest of his book is an attempt to 'cope' with this historical conclusion as a believing Jew.

Sixthly, the resurrection is often supported by appeal to the existence of God. Many people (historians included) object to the resurrection of Christ, not on historical grounds, but on philosophical grounds. They insist that despite the direction in which the historical evidence appears to point, dead people simply do not come back to life; it is a fact of nature. Philosophically, many things can be said about this so called 'naturalistic' objection, and

Professor Richard Swinburne from Oxford University has written a comprehensive critique of it (see the reading list). However, there is a more basic point which deflates the force of the objection.

If there is a God who created all things, raising someone from the dead would hardly be difficult to pull off. The fact that the great majority of Westerners do believe in the existence of God means that, for most of us at least, the resurrection of a person claiming to be God's agent on earth cannot be dismissed simply on the grounds that resurrections cannot happen. If the historical evidence points decisively in the direction of Jesus' resurrection, our belief in the existence of a powerful Creator gets us philosophically 'over the line' or 'into the back of the net', as it were!

Of course, for those that do not accept the existence of God this philosophical reasoning will be of no value. However, such persons are still left with the rather difficult task of explaining how, historically speaking, it looks as though Jesus did rise from the dead.

Conclusion: Christ, the Athenians and the rest of us

I must emphasize again that what I've said in these pages is not intended to 'prove' the Christian faith to you. Whether or not you become a Christian depends not so much on your acceptance of mere facts anyway, but on your willingness to trust your life to the God revealed in Jesus. What I am trying to do here in this book is simply to set out briefly a number of significant lines of verification open to anyone who wants to explore the truthfulness of Christianity. In other words, if you were interested in reading some of the vast literature dedicated to the affirmation of the Christian truth-claim, these are the sorts of issues you can expect to confront.

My central argument throughout these chapters is not that Christianity can be proved and other religions disproved. I have tried instead to pick out what seem to me to be a number of important realities connected with 'spirituality' in the modern world. First, the incurable 'religiosity' of human cultures throughout time illustrates the 'common sense' nature of discussion about God. To ignore the discussion is to stand outside the mainstream of human thought.

Secondly, I have tried to show that the vastly different truth-claims of the world's faiths could not possibly be equally true. Perhaps none of them is true; but the proposition that all of them describe one essential reality is simply indefensible. Tolerance (rightly understood) must exist among peoples, but not at the expense of intellectual integrity.

I have tried, thirdly, to articulate an important distinction between the truth-claims found in the majority of the world's religions and those found in Judaism, Mormonism and Christianity. Hinduism, Buddhism, Sikhism, Islam, Baha'i, and so on, are based on affirmations which cannot be verified. This does not mean that they are necessarily untrue. It means simply that an outside observer is not able with confidence to discern whether or not the claims of, say, Muhammad or Buddha *et al*, are true. It is a matter of pure faith.

As far as I can tell, only three faiths are premised on verifiable claims. The claims of Mormonism, it must be said, do not inspire confidence. Judaism, on the other hand, the forebear of Christianity, grounds itself in events which with some degree of confidence can be said to belong to known history. Most daring of all is the Christian faith—a faith professed by a third of the world today (2.4 billion people). Here, the claims are enormous: God has personally revealed himself (given a photo, if you like) through the Jewish Messiah, Jesus. This man—so the claim goes—is the appointed herald, judge and saviour not just of Jews but of all the peoples of the world. God has given 'assurance' of this by raising this man from the dead—a dramatic, public and verifiable event of ancient history, and one which has shaped the world immeasurably.

When Paul brought his address to a close, climaxing as it did with the news about Christ's resurrection, the reported reactions were various:

> Now when they heard of the resurrection of the dead, some mocked. But others said, "We will hear you again about this." So Paul went out from their midst. But some men joined him and believed, among them Dionysius the Areopagite and a woman named Damaris and others with them.   (ACTS 17:32-33)

I suspect a few of my readers, too, will 'mock' the direction in which this book has headed. This may especially be the case if none of the books listed on page 81 has yet been read. Since this book was not designed to convince anyone of the 'truth' of Christianity I would not regard this outcome as a failure. The only thing I would regard as a failure on my part is if a reader finished this book without developing a curiosity to know more about the claims of Christianity.

On the other hand, there may be a few readers who, like Dionysius and Damaris, find themselves 'believing' in a fresh way. Because I doubt that people come to faith merely through the kind of 'argumentation' presented in this book, I would have to put this down to a delightful miracle (as I'm sure the Apostle Paul did) and would encourage such a reader to look to a more deliberate explanation of the Christian faith such as that found in a number of the books listed on page 81.

My real hope in writing this book is that readers will feel something similar to some of the members of the Areopagus: "We will hear you again about this." I do not mean that I hope you will read more of my books; I simply hope that your spiritual hunches will be aroused enough to find out more about the Christian faith. Again, one way of doing this will be to reflect on some of the books in the suggested reading list. Alternatively, you could surprise a friend by turning up at his or her church, or perhaps just chatting to someone whom you know to believe in Christ. I'm sure you'll find that most Christians are very happy to answer questions about their faith.

I cannot resist the feeling that if God truly wanted our attention he would not offer himself to us in a vague, unverifiable manner: he would, I believe, offer some clarity. He would provide a signpost for the world showing us where to find him. All I am saying is this: why not begin (or perhaps continue) your spiritual pursuit with a closer reading of the 'signposts' of the life, death and resurrection of Jesus Christ?

Paul's speech to the Areopagus (A.D. 50)

Acts 17:16-34

[16]Now while Paul was waiting for them at Athens, his spirit was provoked within him as he saw that the city was full of idols. [17]So he reasoned in the synagogue with the Jews and the devout persons, and in the marketplace every day with those who happened to be there. [18]Some of the Epicurean and Stoic philosophers also conversed with him. And some said, "What does this babbler wish to say?" Others said, "He seems to be a preacher of foreign divinities"— because he was preaching Jesus and the resurrection. [19]And they took hold of him and brought him to the Areopagus, saying, "May we know what this new teaching is that you are presenting? [20]For you bring some strange things to our ears. We wish to know therefore what these things mean." [21]Now all the Athenians and the foreigners who lived there would spend their time in nothing except telling or hearing something new.

[22]So Paul, standing in the midst of the Areopagus, said: "Men of Athens, I perceive that in every way you are very religious. [23]For as I passed along and observed the objects of your worship, I found also an altar with

this inscription, 'To the unknown god.' What therefore you worship as unknown, this I proclaim to you. [24]The God who made the world and everything in it, being Lord of heaven and earth, does not live in temples made by man, [25]nor is he served by human hands, as though he needed anything, since he himself gives to all mankind life and breath and everything. [26]And he made from one man every nation of mankind to live on all the face of the earth, having determined allotted periods and the boundaries of their dwelling place, [27]that they should seek God, in the hope that they might feel their way toward him and find him. Yet he is actually not far from each one of us, [28]for

"'In him we live and move and have our being';

as even some of your own poets have said,

"'For we are indeed his offspring.'

[29]"Being then God's offspring, we ought not to think that the divine being is like gold or silver or stone, an image formed by the art and imagination of man. [30]The times of ignorance God overlooked, but now he commands all people everywhere to repent, [31]because he has fixed a day on which he will judge the world in righteousness by a man whom he has appointed; and of this he has given assurance to all by raising him from the dead."

[32]Now when they heard of the resurrection of the dead, some mocked. But others said, "We will hear you again about this." [33]So Paul went out from their

midst. [34]But some men joined him and believed, among whom also were Dionysius the Areopagite and a woman named Damaris and others with them.

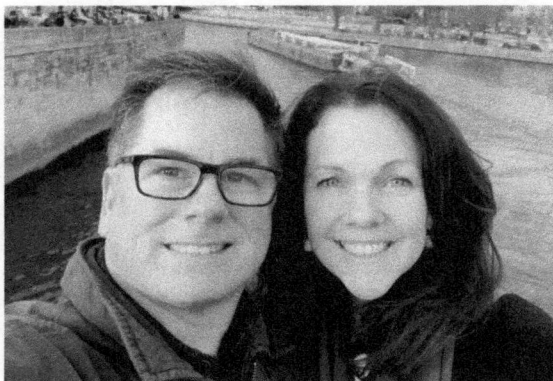

John and Elizabeth ('Buff') Dickson

Resources for further reading

Simple presentations of what Christians believe:

Simply Christianity: A modern guide to the ancient faith by John Dickson, Matthias Media, 1999.
Apologies for the shameless self-promotion. If you want a simple, no-nonsense explanation of the life of Christ this may suit. Alternatively...

Basic Christianity by John Stott, IVP, 2002.
An excellent introduction to the faith for those curious to know what following Christ involves.

Two Ways to Live: The choice we all face.
www.twowaystolive.com
A brief but clear online presentation of the Bible's key themes. Also available in printed form from Matthias Media.

On the question of pluralism and world religions:

Christianity and World Religions: The Challenge of Pluralism by Sir Norman Anderson, IVP, 1984.
An important work by the former Professor of Oriental Laws (specializing in Islamic law) at the University of London. Explores the differences between the world's major religions and the Christian faith.

Jesus Among Other Gods by Ravi Zacharias, Word
Publishing, 2000.
A compelling study of the uniqueness of Christianity
in the light of Buddhism, Islam and Hinduism.

A Spectator's Guide to World Religions by John
Dickson, Aquila Press, 2014.
This book outlines the history, belief systems and
spiritual practices of Hinduism, Buddhism, Judaism,
Christianity and Islam.

On the historicity of Jesus generally:
The Christ Files by John Dickson, Bluebottle
Books, 2006.
A full outline of the historical evidence for Jesus, with
an explanation of how contemporary mainstream
historians assess this evidence.

The Truth About Jesus by P Barnett, Aquila, 1994.
Excellent outline of the historical evidence for Jesus'
life, death and resurrection. Very easy to read.

Who Was Jesus? by NT (Tom) Wright, SPCK, 1992.
From one of the UK's leading New Testament historians,
this book assesses the recent critiques of the biblical
Jesus by such writers as AN Wilson, Barbara Thiering
and John Spong. Very readable and compelling.

A Doubter's Guide to Jesus by John Dickson, Zondervan, 2018.
This is an introduction to the major portraits of Jesus
found in the earliest historical sources.

On the resurrection of Christ in particular:

Did Jesus Rise From The Dead? The Resurrection Debate by Gary Habermas and Antony Flew (edited by Terry L Miethe), Harper & Row, 1987.

On 2-3 May 1985, the philosophy faculty of Liberty University, Virginia USA, hosted a professionally adjudicated debate between the renowned scholar and atheist, Professor Antony Flew, and an expert in the origins of Christianity, historian Dr Gary Habermas. The topic of the debate was "The Historicity of the Resurrection: Did Jesus Rise from the Dead?" The transcripts of the debate together with additional comments from a variety of scholars appear in this book.

The Historicity of the Empty Tomb of Jesus
www.leaderu.com/offices/billcraig/docs/tomb2.html
An important online article by a leading historian and philosopher, Professor William Lane Craig.

On some of the wider arguments for Christianity:

The Reason for God by Tim Keller, Penguin, 2008.
Keller uses literature, philosophy and real-life conversations to explain how it is soundly rational to have faith in the Christian God.

The Problem of God by Mark Clark, Zondervan, 2017.
This is written by a skeptic who became a Christian and then a pastor, all while exploring answers to the most difficult questions raised against Christianity.

Philosophers Who Believe edited by KJ Clark, IVP, 1993.
Professional academic philosophers tell of their own faith in Christ. Excellent for anyone with an interest in philosophical queries about faith.

The Existence of God by Richard Swinburne, Clarendon Press, 1991.
As the title suggests, this is a full-scale demonstration of the existence of God and related philosophical issues. It is not for the novice, but if you are someone or know someone with high level philosophical doubts about the reality of God, this is the book to read.

Also by John Dickson

Simply Christianity
A modern guide to the ancient faith

One of the reasons people sometimes avoid looking into Christianity is that there are so many versions on offer, each with its own religious package. The project of this book is to get beyond the rituals, myth and dogma. By going back to the earliest biographies of Jesus—the Gospels in the New Testament—*Simply Christianity* finds what remains after the 'religion' is stripped away. It's a great book for understanding the core of Christian faith.

FOR MORE INFORMATION OR TO ORDER CONTACT:

Matthias Media	Matthias Media (USA)
Email: sales@matthiasmedia.com.au	Email: sales@matthiasmedia.com
www.matthiasmedia.com.au	www.matthiasmedia.com

Also by John Dickson

If I were God, I'd end all the pain
Struggling with evil, suffering and faith

Why doesn't God do something about all the pain and suffering? Why does he let it happen? In fact, can we still believe in God in the face of all the evil in the world?

In this book, John Dickson looks honestly at these questions and provides some compelling biblical answers. He looks briefly at the alternative explanations for suffering provided by Hinduism, Buddhism, Islam and Atheism, shows why the perspective of the Bible is the best one available, and points finally to Christ's death and the gospel of mercy as God's answer to our suffering world.

FOR MORE INFORMATION OR TO ORDER CONTACT:

Matthias Media
Email: sales@matthiasmedia.com.au
www.matthiasmedia.com.au

Matthias Media (USA)
Email: sales@matthiasmedia.com
www.matthiasmedia.com